Wagging around in Scandinavia 2016

This journal, which will be extracts from the diary I kept, and some of the photos, is for anyone who is interested. Lots of people get discouraged from adventure by various things, various people, and I want to say to anyone thinking of it, don't listen to the pessimists and don't take any notice of the gear snobs. Most of the gear fanatics spend their time buying expensive stuff and talking about it. While that may apply in a country without any bicycle shops, in a country that does have bike shops you don't necessarily need an expensive bike. The trips I have taken testify to that. Travelling by bicycle is the cheapest way.

Having already cycled Norway's west coast I went this time for Sweden's east coast, on the Baltic, crossing Finland into north Norway. A good customer gave me a bike. The other stuff I took was my light panniers, a travel bag, bungee straps, 2 women's handbags tied on the front, 1 man tent, good sleeping bag, layers of ordinary clothes, not too many, waterproof. Etc. I decided to get the 21 gear Claud Butler touring bike to Sweden by ferry and train.

hook of Holland

12 July 2016

Take train from Taunton to Paddington; pissing wet day, cross London, wait around at Liverpool Street, take train to Harwich. Get on night ferry to Hook of Holland – that's the grey photo. Harwich was equally depressing, perhaps slightly worse. Some wet clothes and a very wet ferry ticket. Trains not that user friendly for bikes and gear, I had to have bags all bungeed together, bung the bike in the guards van then leg it back down the platform onto the train.

13 July

Train to Amsterdam, plenty space for bike, just wheeled it on and stayed with it. Spoke to a few people, including ticket collector. Cycled around a bit in Amsterdam, quite hectic, everybody gives way to beautiful people. General rule. Let it appear as if you're not looking where you're going.

Girls in tourist office too busy unless you're looking for an expensive hotel. Probably best do some research before getting there. I found a place called Hotel Washington a little ride from town. A little attic room with a double bed up 3 flights of steep stairs. 87 Euros. Like I said, book before going to Amsterdam. The man says no smoking in hotel anymore, 'although there is a little balcony...' He seems Jewish. For sure he's the son of a Jew. 'Although it depends on the quantity,' he adds, 'obviously if it's industrial quantities, you know, like a chillum, or those bongs shaped like skulls...' There's no stopping him as he launches into whimsy; eventually I manage to ask about the bike. 'Oh yes you can bring it through the back, probably best leave it a while though as we're pretty jammed up at the moment.'

There's a little kettle in my room, and sure enough there is a little balcony, but I don't feel like getting stoned. I've already booked a ticket to Hamburg for the following morning, and am intent on making progress.

When I go back down the son of a Jew is outside where all the hotel bikes are kept on the street, mine amongst them: 'Ah, there you are. Is this your bike? I thought it must be. It's kind of in the way.' I wheel it through the kitchen into a small courtyard that looks like a bicycle burial ground. 'Have a pleasant evening.' He says, suggestively.

Amsterdam

Thurs 14 July

What I forgot to mention about the ferry was the racism incident. I think it's worth recording. It's one of the moments that, for the bystander, easily slips by, unless recorded.

A Dutch man brought a steward to accost an Indian man who was sitting with his family at one of the bars. 'Did you take photos in the children's play area?' Was the question repeated several times. I think the Indian man was asking what he wanted. 'Can I see the photos please.' This was all loud enough to attract a small crowd. The Indian man got out his camera and his family stood up looking bewildered. I stood up as well, I'd never seen a paedophile before and I thought it could be interesting to see one in the flesh. I suppose that's what everyone else was thinking. But when I saw him I was confused, and I saw that he was confused as well.

Then I looked at the accuser and his aid, the steward. I saw repressed hatred in one, judicious austerity in the other. Then I felt embarrassed and ashamed and left. So I didn't see the outcome. Sorry about that. A disappointing piece of journalism that was. What I guess happened was that it all fizzled out awkwardly. What I find interesting, though, is the reaction of the Indian man. Not his wife or children. They were just bewildered. No, he alone, against an onslaught of accusation and suggestion remained calm, respectful, and I would say dignified, though my cultural upbringing would give dignity a certain pique, a slight rufflement, a barely discernible impatience. I saw only humility.

Afterwards, away from the scene, I wondered whether maybe the accusations had some ground. Maybe this sort of thing is happening all the time: men take photos/videos; Indian men take photos/videos of children's play areas on ferries and unscrupulously sell them on the internet. After all if Rolf Harris could anyone could. But it occurred to me that maybe he concealed his embarrassment or anger in order to avoid looking guilty, wanting the moment to pass by as painlessly as possible. But why oh why did he not say: 'How dare you insult me you racist, paranoid, fascist potato eaters.'

Answers on a postcard please.

And a part of me thought: serve you right you smug, amoral, non-committal, elusive, unrufflable Indian. You so spiritually superior you won't even enter into the affray of western philosophy. And I caught myself drifting into the comfort of the Dutch clan, the white clan, the European home.

But I was thinking of the children in Delhi saying: 'No photo, no photo.' At first I was bewildered, then I realised that what I was trying to capture was poverty and a sort of beauty in poverty, which is quite a fashionable commodity – the postcards of the mother in rags, or the wrinkly old man with his chickens, or oiling the wheels of his rickshaw. Which is a kind of invasion, a disrespectful sort of voyeurism. I put the camera away. I was photographing 'them'. Now they, or at least the oligarchs amongst them, are photographing 'us'. And we are saying: 'No photo. No photo.'

Continuing with the story – train to Hamburg. All the platforms at Amsterdam have elevators and lifts to them. I thought I'd try going up an elevator. It seemed pretty straightforward, just hold the bike while you go up. But getting onto the first step was the problem - I tumbled back down only to be carried forward again in a clumsy pickle. I think it was all the baggage. I realised I was no longer making rational decisions. The stress causing crowds were taking their toll. I had to stay alert. At Osnabrook station in Germany I thought I'd entered a Nazi time warp and every time I looked at the dirty clock on the platform it had only moved five minutes. Always five minutes. Finally as the train came in an overweight, moustachioed, probably wife beating guard stopped me to examine my tickets. He was deliberately slow and obfuscatory. Perhaps he'd noticed the way I looked at him – as a 1930's caricature, but he didn't like my tickets. Then I had to run to get on at the front of the train.

Hamburg. I go straight to the ticket office. I'm getting used to the system now. You queue for a ticket with a number. When your number comes up you go to a desk. You wait and wait and hope that the desk you end up at won't be the one with the miserable reptilian woman sitting behind it.

But what you don't realise is she's the best. She secretly likes to be the quickest and best. She's the no nonsense, tired, doesn't like scruffy foreigners kind of woman. She doesn't like to be beaten. I take my ticket for Copenhagen and head for the tourist office. I've decided to hide the yellow fluorescent waistcoat and use the line: 'I'm looking for a hotel.' The girl quickly finds me somewhere in the Bronx of Hamburg.

Significantly cheaper than the hotel in Amsterdam. However the concierge wouldn't let me take my bike in no matter how much I pleaded. I said it was a very dangerous place for my bike outside. He said it wasn't just mine it was everybody's. He suggested a place I leave the bike, but I took it back to the station instead, locked it up there. Imagined him and his mates looking around for it and cursing. There was a complimentary bottle of water in my room, but with a 4 Euro price tag on it. That got me thinking. I refilled it from the tap. I haven't felt so naughty since I stole sweets from the vicar's daughter. Somehow I knew it was right.

Then I went out, drank beer and ate pork and red cabbage. Nice place almost opposite the railway station.

Fri 15 july

Feeling a bit tetchy six twenty five waiting to go into breakfast room at hotel Bronx of hamburg. No way is it possible to go in five minutes early. The woman at reception looks down again only when I've moved away from the door. At precisely six thirty she looks up again and inclines her head.

Pleased to see the bike is still where I left it. It's also early enough that the station is not too crowded. But it's cold and grey and reminds me that we are all waiting for death. Keeping ourselves busy until we come to places like this. When my train comes I step onto it gladly and let the doors close behind me. Two guards come through talking, they smile. And that's enough for me to be glad to be aboard for the next leg.

Copenhagen; I've realised how far it all is. I thought I'd jump on a train, have a little sleep and before death occurred I'd have arrived in Stockholm. i did a lot of looking out the window and thinking while the train rattled through Germany and then Denmark. I thought about work for a bit, what had been and what would be or might be; then I thought about how Denmark looked very similar to Germany, then about women, particularly one woman, and then I let my thoughts free wheel until they weren't thoughts at all. At one point two police men walked through and looked at everyone. Then the train rattled on until late in the afternoon when Copenhagen never seemed to stop arriving.

A man with two bikes tells me to try the back packers hostel near the station, then he disappears up the escalator while I go to find the out of order lift. And then there are people everywhere, every step you take.

Maybe it's because I'm tired but am beginning to dislike the people that work at the ticket offices. Sure it's a stressful job but I'm sure they hate us even more than we hate them. It's impossible to take a bike by train to Stockholm. I say it's already been done I read about it. Nothing. Just piss off on your bike. I don't think they fully appreciate the nature of the expedition that I am undertaking. Let's see how we get on with the people at malmo tomorrow.

I have a walk around then head back to the hostel for a beer before bed. I go out to the beer garden out the back and there's a group of young travellers sitting around a picnic table. They're greasy exhibitionists around a mouthy female, but apart from that they're quite amiable and they start to befriend me when I come back with my second pint. Then a nervous young new Zealander tags along and when they close up the garden we end up perched on bar stools and he tells me about his plans to sow his seeds around Europe. Probably the beer, but I start feeling queasy, so when he heads off to hit the town I slowly climb through the labyrinth to my dorm. There I meet my room mates, some of whom are just about to go out. The others are just lying on their bunks fiddling with their phones. I clamber up the ladder onto my bed and lie there with my book in my hand and I know that if I'm not sick I'm certainly in for an uncomfortable night.

Sat 16 july

While I wasn't sleeping I wondered whether it was
the beer after all that made me feel sick, whether it
was the edgy new Zealander, or whether it was that
bof sandwich I'd bought from the dippy old lady at
the street stall. Half of my room mates returned
shortly before grey daylight started filtering through
the blinds of one big window. They whispered and
they whispered. Then they went quiet and snored.
At six the others got up, packed up loudly, showered
and left. Then it was quiet and I kept my eyes closed
and concentrated on an image I had of a Norwegian
fjord lit crimson in sunrise.

Malmo is like a ghost town compared with
Copenhagen. At the ticket office I don't bother
asking about getting to Stockholm I just buy a ticket
for Jonkoping on a regional train. I have a cycle
around. It's deserted. Not at all as I remember it.
Then I sit inside the station in the afternoon waiting
for the train as it starts to rain. A young black man
comes and sits beside me, a born again Christian,
keeps asking me if I'll repent my sins. Eventually he
walks away in disgust and a sympathetic bystander

comes to speak. He's Swedish, an ex-truck driver who's travelling around the country by train. He hasn't decided where he's heading next so he is sat at the station having a think. Nice guy. Jonkoping, he tells me, has the biggest lake in Sweden.

Its evening. I cycle alongside the lake, find a grassy place in amongst some small rowan trees and pitch the tent. My first night outdoors, such a relief.

Jonkoping

Sun 17 july

Back to Jonkoping for a train to nassjo and then
norjoping. Am accosted by a team of begging
Bulgarian women. That's at Jonkoping before I leave
on the first train. Give the first one some change,
then give the second one the rest of my change,
some of which she throws to the ground shouting;
'this no good, this Danish, this no good to me, no

want this rubbish.' Meanwhile the first woman is trying to sell me a gold ring which is 20 carrot and belonged to her grandmother. I put it back in her cup and wave the others away. But still they whine on; 'pleeze pleeze give me money, give me 200 krona, for food, we are hungry, have no money, sleep on street, pleeze pleeze I beg you just give me money... until I have to wave my arms at them like they are seagulls whilst walking away, and one; 'I'll remember how kind, how generous the English can be, from your rich country...'

I notice that the other travellers ignore the women completely as if they don't exist.

On the train I meet a teacher who shares some fudge and cherries with me and we strike up a long conversation, changing trains together all the way to Norjoping. Then he gets his bike and leads me to the outskirts of the town.

After all the train travel it feels like a long hard ride to nykoping and it's getting dim as I buy some more food and water in a supermarket on the edge of town. It's a big town with seemingly endless paved pedestrian streets lined with restaurants. On the northern side of town I find a hillock away from the cycle path, under pine trees, and erect the tent amongst blueberries. I eat some and think again about those Bulgarian women and their menfolk, unseen, somewhere else, picking cherries along the roadside, rummaging through bins or smoking in the town squares.

Mon 18 july

I didn't mention the lovely Swedish girl I met the day before yesterday, also travelling with bike on train from malmo. That's because she slipped my mind, which is odd considering that she was a kindred spirit and we talked for probably an hour. She'd tied a rucksack onto her carrier as a makeshift pannier and I helped her attach her pump to the bike frame with insulation tape. she told me about the campsite at Stockholm and wrote down the name on my map. That's my target for today. And I have my own road parallel with the motorway. It's almost empty and gently undulates mile after hot mile past blue meadows and fields of rape. By mid afternoon I reach the coast and Stockholm still seems a long way away. Anna texts asking when I'm going to fly to Italy and I say in about a month. 'Ok take care.' I know that means she's pissed off.

Its late afternoon as I cycle into the outskirts of the city and get on a commuter train; heading the opposite way to most of the people. I get off south of the centre and try to find the campsite. With directions from several people I eventually find it. It's a quiet haven close to the water with all the usual - toilets, showers, kitchen. Beats an expensive hotel in the city anytime. Once I've recovered a bit from the days ride I cycle into town looking for internet cafes, but they a thing of the past I'm told what with these fancy phones everyone's got. I get a beer and sit outside on a quiet road; immigrants unload a lorry up the street and I watch all the rich as they go out to eat and drink. 6.50 for the beer, and I'm pondering what these immigrants will do when winter arrives. Am feeling tetchy as I head back to the campsite to cook a late meal. Anna's gone silent and I wonder whether she's given up on me after my decision to head north. All the people on the streets are mindless cattle, mobiles plumbed to their waists at the intersection of torn jeans, or tight jeans. True some of them are beautiful, but many of them are fat. Not as fat as English people though. And they like overtaking you on the cycle paths just like in Amsterdam, no matter how fast you're going they have to pass the traveller.

Tue 19 july

Hot and clear, feel rested, decide to stay another night and explore the city. At the university library they let me use a computer for thirty minutes and I email a short letter to Anna. Getting the hang of cycling round – very user friendly cycle city, paths everywhere, feels safe. It's beautiful on the waterfronts with views across to the islands; majestic old buildings everywhere and grand squares. But it's too hot and I have to head back to the campsite to read my book. Onto second book; wolf hall relegated to firelighting.

In the evening meet a nice German couple in their late thirties who are doing a round the world cycle trip.

Wed 20 july

Leave Stockholm. get to Gavle by train then cycle on through endless miles of pine and birch forest. Great. No rivers or lakes though, just forest on bog and an undulating road. I stop near a wooden village and go down a forest track for a short break. While I'm eating blueberries and sultanas and studying the map a guy exercising a horse with a trap races past and returns a few minutes later again and again until I head back for the road and meet another guy on a tractor driving in. feels like a strange place that doesn't like outsiders. head on towards a river I can see on the map but when I get to it it's a muggy dark place thick with mosquitoes. There's a private English type park behind an old stone wall. I fill up with water and move on. After another hour I go down a road to meet the coast. Where the tarmac ends there's about 100 camper vans parked in a carpark. There's a jetty and an expensive restaurant and some boats. And there are some signs saying no camping. But there's a beautiful view across the Baltic; it's cooler, free of insects and the trees on the islands are deep green against the light blue sky.

baltic

Thurs 21

Last night I found a campsite with a beautiful little
beach and today I can't drag myself away. The place
is near a paper mill but that doesn't seem to bother
anyone; the wind's blowing the smells the opposite
way. It's hot and the water at the sandy beach
nearby is warm enough to stay in a while. try fishing
but no luck with spinners or sultanas or bread. No
bait to be found anywhere. No signs of limpets or
muscles or anything which is a bit worrying, though
the water looks clean. Then an arab family turn up at
the beach with lots of screaming children. Everyone
else leaves. I stay on a while, but then go back to the
campsite with its own stony beach and read my
book there. By the evening have nearly finished the
book, which was by far too easy a read, one of those
pacy thrillers that I didn't mind leaving behind.
Trouble is after that there'll be nothing else to read.
I may have to write more whimsy, these pacy
thrillers are like sweets that melt in the mouth and
leave one undernourished, and slightly annoyed.

Fri 22

Cycle to hudiksval . ask at the station café if they'll
fill my water bottles, they won't. I should have
bought a coffee or something but I wanted to know
what it feels like being an economic refugee. I still
don't know but am inwardly ranting on the train all
the way to sundsval. Am really making progress

now, making up for lost time, heading north. It's an intercity train not a regional and the guard was a nice old guy, not like some of the gestapoesque lady guards, who let me on even though he shouldn't have and charged me a very reasonable nominal sum of 100 krona. He understood. From sundsval it's busy on the coast and the way to timra is a maze of cycle paths and lucky routes through coastal retirement villages. In hindsight it would have been better to have headed inland before now. When it starts getting late I camp in some pine woods between the motorway and a railway line with a poor looking housing estate beside it. It's noisy but I'm safely hidden amongst the heather.

Sat 23

Cycle to harnosand. Have to go inland via stigsjo. On
the coast it's the e4 or nothing and I spend a long
time trying to negotiate out of the bermuda triangle
area around timra airport. In the end it's a nice ride,
quite hilly and winding. Stop for lunch by a river
make tea and lentil soup with rice. Got a craving for
liquorice. In the afternoon I take a train from
harnosand to umea, which is quite a way north on
the Baltic, and a big city. Why I am in such a rush I
can explain because the texting with the Italian
beauty I met in june has resumed and now there are
2 pulls to get north – that lonely crimson fjord I
remember from 2009 being one.

Umea is an attractive city with a big pedestrian high
street and a big river with a cycle path alongside it
and lots of cycle bridges everywhere going over
roads and water and train tracks. There's a triathlon
in progress as I cycle along the riverside and I end up
in amongst crowds of spectators for a while, but
then I leave them behind further down river towards
the estuary and the university. The university
campus is huge, on its own hill above the river and

the main city, northwards. It's a maze of cycle paths and there's more water and forest beyond, and a sandy beach with pine trees either side of it. I camp there, invisible from the beach.

Finish the pacy thriller. Entertaining, but a disappointing ending. The secret history by donna tartt. Guess not her real name. insisted on giving a final run down of the futures of all the peripheral characters, including the pets, I skipped to the last paragraph and that was that. She likes putting herself into the male character, does it very well, shows all their vanities, weaknesses, etc. one thing I did notice though – the one female heroine comes out looking pretty good.

Sun 24 july

navigation seems to come more naturally after a good nights sleep among the trees. dawn brings warmth and birdsong and midges. Probably the most painless crossing of a city ever, skirting around the northern edge by compass following the cycle paths finding by chance the road to Botsmark; no getting stuck on busy roads with lorries and coaches chuffing, no roundabouts or traffic lights to risk, no

lane changing road hogging required. Ersmark, 364.
a lovely smooth road through pine forest. Peat bog.
Unmanaged or managed for pulpwood only,
management by proxy – regular exploitation. A
slash and move on. Dont knock it if it works.
Forestry's hard and dangerous why not do it like
that? Like extracting minerals from a moonscape.
Cushioned in heated cabs that perch, abdomen like,
amidst great hydraulic appendages that crush or
compact everything before them - for the pulp mills
on the coast, hungry machines, for all the pizza
boxes. You can tell where they are by the smoke and
the timber lorries laden. And thats good. Thats
everybody busy. us keeping up with them.

Today I ran right out of water and got a bit
dehydrated in the heat. Kept looking at all the
muddy pools and wondering when to make that
desperate move - stop, light a fire and boil the
brown peaty stuff. Eventually though, like a reward,
I came to a beautiful river with grass, a firebox a
little hut with wood stored for fishermen. Camped
there and made endless cups of tea and a big meal
of rice and lentils. And slept.

by the river

Baltic sea at Umea

Mon 25 july

It's hard leaving an oasis. Got to within 20km of Jorn. There's a station there, and shops. Stopped by a still lake, all overgrown around the edge. On the side of the road an old grassy layby. lit a fire there and managed it carefully, cooked spaghetti and lentils. lay in the shade of late afternoon for a long time apathetic toward going on. When I got to Jorn I thought there might be a train but I'd missed it. Decided to head on toward the next stop. Tired and saddle sore, but I'd found a rhythm. Trouble was I couldn't see anywhere to camp and it was getting late. Prerequisites are: water, flat dry place, fuel. Plenty of wood around. Not the others. Eventually found another lake and a beautiful view. I couldn't get enough of that view after all those miles of swampy forest. And found a crevice for the tent amongst some blueberries. I was eating them and getting eaten by midges. I put the tent up, smeared on the insect repellant and went to sit and look at the view across the lake - low mountains and rolling forest.

Tue 26

didn't sleep aswell as expected ontop of the
blueberries. Got up, ate some more berries, sultanas
and biscuits and headed on toward Alvesby. All the
stations on route were closed and overgrown. The
trains just fly through them. Another gruelling day of
saddlesoreness but I was getting used to it, it wasn't
too hilly, and the wind was behind me. A lot of the
day I was going parallel with the railway line but I
only saw one train. And then I realised why I was
making such good progress. It wasn't just the wind
that was behind me it was a storm. A bloody great
storm full of thunder and lightening was right behind
me and I still wasn't getting wet. Just getting blown
along infront of it. I came down a long hill out of
thick forest into pasture lands where there was a
long thin lake. I saw someone else with a bike
putting on his waterproofs but I careered on while
the going was good. And then I came up against a
wall of wind coming from ahead and the storm
behind me caught up. Then it rained. Really hard and
I didn't bother putting on my water proof as I was

sticky with sweat and enjoying the cold shower. I just stowed away my t-shirt, put my flourescent waistcoat on and put the waterproof sacks over my paniers. The storm didn't know which way it was going but I did and rode head down against the wind along the main road to Alvesby. There were major roadworks on the way and lines of traffic at least 10 cars long! New tarmac was being laid and the road was steaming. At Alvesby I was shivering and had to put dry clothes on, found the nearest big COOP store and bought some more food. Bananas, milk and liquorice. Bread, cheese, ham, bottled water, and I gave an old 50 krone note to the Bulgarian tramp outside. Out of date. But apparently the banks would change it. Then I went to the station and sheltered from the rain. The next train was in three hours time at nine.

When the rain stopped the sun came out and I left the station and explored the town. After about 20 minutes I found I was loitering in the park overlooking the town. There I met a guy who was walking along with a can of beer on his way to 'the mountain' for a smoke. He asked me if I'd like to join him and I said I didn't have time as I had a train to catch in a few hours. But I'd be happy to have a smoke with him there. So he went away for his home stash of what he said was mild stuff and was back within five minutes.

He had five children, he told me, with a Ugandan woman who he'd met while he was still at school, and she subsequently, to cut things short, after another visit, meeting the parents, discussion of his intentions, etc moved to Sweden and lived with him and his parents. I think my jaw was hanging low so he went on to explain things more; she easily got a visa because his father wrote to guarantee that she would be living under his care and wouldn't be a burden to the state. He went on to explain why he thought his father was so liberal, and I think it was then that it struck me how intimate a conversation we were having, how open and uninhibited. Also that I was taking everything in but unable to speak coherently.

His feelings for his father were nothing short of admiration. Then we leaned back against the bench on which we sat and enjoyed the view in tranquil silence. Then the conversation went in directions I can't remember. He was only still in his 20's had 5 children and was exceedingly calm. He was trying, he told me, to break out of his shyness, to feel free to make a connection, to not be an island. How special meetings with strangers can be as an opportunity to do that, we both agreed. And I think there was for both of us a sense of wonder. It started raining again and he went home, it being too late to go to the mountain now, not that he regretted it, not by any means, and there was where he lived and I could always visit him if I came back. That added a breath of wind to the cloud I was floating on. I was genuinely moved and felt that my invocations of pleasure had been insufficient in there ardency. And I was sorry for that. I considered going back to try to better express my agreement with what he'd said, but thought better of it and coasted back to the station not at all confident of my direction.

There I fell seamlessly into a long disjointed conversation with a young Russian traveller whose only luggage was a plastic bag. He was very smartly dressed, and his pullover, he said, was in the bag. I think I was as amazed by him as he was by me. How brave we both thought the other was. Only a plastic bag I kept saying, travelling to Norway by bicycle, he kept saying. we shook hands warmly, twice infact because my train was delayed. I was exhausted after all that socialising, looking forward to a quiet sit down on a comfortable train. Rummaging around looking for my phone charger when the ticket collecter came. I turned around expecting to see one of those Stasi type women, but there stood a beautiful young woman dressed in blue and white uniform looking at me with twinkling green eyes. She was blonde, petite and eager to talk, and led me down to her little office on the train. As she showed me photos of her elk hunting expeditions, fishing, mountaineering, etc on her phone I was wondering how long I could get away with just grunting and nodding, how I really wanted to go back, sit down, put my phone on charge and stare out of the window. But she was enchanting and I told her how pleasantly surprised I was to find an attractive young woman made up like a townie girl, but who also enjoyed getting out there and doing the real thing. Shyness was kicking back in - safe, protective, civilised shyness. She smiled ever so sweetly, almost dangerously, before I shook her hand and stalked back to my seat.

It was late when the train arrived at Boden. I cycled north until I found a field to camp in, out of site.

the road behind

t

he road infront

Friday 29 july

am getting confused with the recapping and it
doesn't much matter what day it is. It's today NOW
and i've really made some progress thanks to that
bit of cheating I did with the trains. Infact am not far
south of Muoni, on the Finnish border. It's still forest
but not quite so swampy. There's willow and a river
here; i've decided to stop and stay at this bothy. The
hail's hammering on the tin roof as I sit infront of the
fire on the veranda. Inside looks a bit like a summer

house with furniture. Glass doors, wooden floor, another fireplace so you can have a fire inside and or outside. Inspite of the wood floor and furniture i'd say a 2 star bothy compared with some of the Scottish ones, but a lot better than my little tent.

Arrived here just in time to shelter from another storm. It's 5 O'clock. No way am I going on now. Got food on the fire and clothes drying. Food's expensive here even in supermarkets. The other reason why I'm living largely on rice and lentils is because it packs small and gives you several days eating. When you stop taking trains the shops are a long way apart. Today the roads weren't too bad, just one 2km stretch unsurfaced. But yesterday was a day of cycling in hell. no. the day before yesterday and yesterday were cycling days from hell and I think I was too depressed to write. That's why this gap has appeared. Am guessing about 30 km of unsurfaced road with those big stones they use to lay under asphalt. Hot swampy pine scrubland with no rivers and nowhere to stop, just trudging on mile after mile with cars going past occasionally - raising up the dust. And then another similar day after because they don't believe in doing short stretches of road at a time here. No clean water anywhere just a dusty stony road to walk along forever. My first puncture also. Settle down in the dirt at the edge of the road to fix it. If I could have beamed away from that I would. If I could have stepped into a parallel dimension where that didn't happen I would have, and would never have regretted any loss of character building it might have necessitated. For I don't believe now I am any better off for it. Or do I. After that I don't expect a lot, and this spooky oasis seems like paradise.

What a relief it was to be back on smooth tarmac with the road slipping away under me again and the trees gliding by more like a blur than a constant reminder of what a lack of planning can bring. But what is an adventure without a lack of planning? 9 Oclock in the evening Pajala was like a derelict ghost town. A hamburger bar was open and there was a line of people sat at the steamed up window stuffing their fat pasty faces and STARING OUT INTO NOTHING. I thought i'd transposed into some similar version of invasion of the body snatchers. Does that sound judgemental? There are a lot of overweight people here. And that's that. The forest is all swamp scrub harvested for pulp by the big money; what else is there to do but eat? I'm sorry this is a negative period.

The coop is always open. And I love the coop. There you feel safe. Everything is normal. You look at food. Other people look at food. Everybody eats. We've got that in common. Then I got the hell out of there and continued north. And after a while gave up trying to find a nice place to camp and settled for an oversized but underused road stone storage area. And there had a surprisingly good nights sleep.

Sun 31

Didn't sleep so well at the bothy as expected. The wood floor was harder than the surfaces I was used to and I kept hearing noises which could have been people but weren't. Was half expecting a gang of drunk youths to arrive on a drugs binge or a trash and burn fest.

At five I got up feeling stiff, cold and gloomy. A thick damp mist swallowed the whole place. Dew and fog hanging timeless. I made tea and a spaghetti breakfast. Tired, and still saddle sore the prospect of another gruelling ride through swampy forest darkened the morning which didn't get light even when I left. The Italian lady was texting me wanting my projected flight date and I was sorely tempted to say I was right on my way, where's the nearest airport? Nowhere near here came the silent answer out of the forest.

But I was going north flying through the mist, beads of dew collecting in my woollen jumper. By mid morning the wind had turned against me and I was really struggling. It was sunny and then cloudy and then raining and then sunny again. Like that. That last 50 miles to Karesuando at the top of Sweden, was all slog on long undulating roads with occasional bends and then more of the same. But the views were getting better. At the tops of each hill you could see out over the forest. That was more interesting than just having reddish stems constantly sliding by.

Karesuando – the gateway to Finland – is a tourist hotspot. It's where all the travellers go to hang about. They were there in all shapes and colours, in luxury vans or bumming along on foot – sandals hanging from pack. There were tents pitched outside the tourist office and every sign of the beginnings of a music festival. There were crowds of locals milling around wondering if they needed another t-shirt. In the tourist office I easily got on the internet . Ironic really that I had better access to the internet at the top of Sweden than at the bottom. The one shop there had the usual array of expensive bread, salami and chorizo . Although saying that probably not so expensive as a single shop in a tourist village in Britain.

Finland

Norway

It rained a bit and I waited outside the tourist office
eating bread and ham and bananas and drinking
milk. Wonderful milk. Then I got moving as a band
started tuning up, took some photos at the bridge
on the border and went on into Finland. Left turn
towards the Norwegian coast. Music receding. No
officials in site no need to show passport. Mountains
in the distance, clean rivers and birch scrub. Rock
and heather. And blueberries. About 8 pm dark
clouds were following me so I pulled off and went

down a little track towards a lake, but there were 2 campers parked there and loads of noisy kids. One of the Dads was attempting some fishing, got his line caught on the first cast. Easily done, I lost some tackle at the bothy caught it in a tree and never got it all back. No one acknowledged my existence, and as I looked around for a possible pitch site they carried on as if I weren't there. They didn't want anyone else there and I didn't want them to be there. And that's because there are too many people. Too many people in the nice places. He said wistfully.

As I rode on I turned around. About 500m behind in the exact place on that lake where the campers and their kids had parked, rain was sheeting down out of the low cloud like death rays from an alien ship. I turned back and hurried on, feeling only a little sympathy. But the rain didn't get as far as me – spent itself on the German campers. I went on in sunshine, but when I found a place by a river on higher ground I put the tent up quick and got all my stuff in before I lit a fire, before I attempted to light a fire. For it was after several fruitless attempts that I finally got something smouldering and then this car came rumbling down the track to the river and stopped by my tent. A man got out. We looked at each other. I said 'Am I OK camped here?' 'OK' he said 'I come to wash hair.' 'Right' I said 'OK' \There was a bit of a pause in which it was obvious we were entirely comfortable with each other. I wondered why of all the places he could have chosen to wash his hair he decided to do it here. 'Is it special water?' I asked him. 'Is special water , yes' he replied, with the faintest trace of irony to match my faint provocation. He was late fifties, big build, receding hair. He brought a big 2 handled metal bucket from the back of his rusty car. 'Good water.' That was a straightforward assertion. 'Clean?' I asked. 'Good to drink?' 'Yes it is clean. Good to drink. Where are you from?' 'I'm from England.' 'Where in England?' 'The south west, in the country. It's a very different kind of country but I live in the country.' 'I am with the reindeer from further north.' 'Oh, are you Sami?' 'Sami yes I am Sami.'We come to Norway in the summer go to Sweden in the winter with the animals.' 'Ah that would explain why i've seen reindeer in Sweden with collars. Would they be animals that escaped?' I glanced at the barely smoking fire. 'The mosquitoes,' he said by way of explanation. Then he went briskly down to the river. i turned to my fire while he pulled off his shirt and started pouring bucket loads of water over his head on the grass near the river; he stepped away a pace or two from the river every time. When he finished he beamed with satisfaction. 'Is good.' he said. 'Refreshing,' I said. Then he went off to the music festival. He must know all the good hair washing spots -I thought – as he revved and rattled off down the road. That was a nice spot, a bit barren, but very comfortable.

Then this morning the rain was still pattering on the tent when I got up and stuffed everything away and stretched the pannier sacks over the panniers and ate some biscuits and hurriedly made tea with the meths stove. And then a gentle uphill slog in constant foggy drizzle, about 60 miles to a place in the mountains with an unpronounceable name. There was a delux visitor centre, with plug in points and clean toilets. I hung about in there trying to warm up until the woman said she was closing – it was only 3.30, so I went on to the foodstore which was surprisingly big and full of people. Usual dour shop girls. Even more cold when I came out and I was wearing t-shirt under shirt under jumper under fleece, but the rain had stopped and beyond the Norwegian border it was all beautiful, downhill, following a steeply falling river. A mystical, hypnotic, musical river, clean turquoise. Towards the coast. Beside that river I camped, lit a big fire and stared at the scenery until it was time to sleep.

Mon 1 aug

11 am. Still here by the river, which is still gurgling and humming out its unfinished symphony. Lying here in the horizontal in this rapidly getting wet tent. Sometimes I lie on my back and sometimes I lie on my side. Eat some biscuits. Drink some more water. Go out for a piss, which involves getting more water in than is already dripping in down at the foot end. Such a decision must be thought through. Its the steady wetting kind of rain that doesn't abate, just drums down on the tent roof relentlessly. I could pack up and go but then i'd get soaked before I started and that could be a problem. Because it's not warm. No it's a cold rain that falls in this valley.

That was this morning. About 3 it stopped for just long enough for me to pack up. Then it resumed again similar to before. Head down and waterproofed up I got past skibotn and onto the coast road with a strong headwind . Once on the coast it really started chucking down and my thick woollen socks were waterlogged and lorries were thundering by sending up walls of spray. The sea slid by in a too slow blur of grey wateriness. Oh to be back on those unsurfaced roads in hot Sweden, I was thinking. What a nightmare. For the umpteenth time I thought: this isn't fun. I stopped in a layby with a view of windswept sea on one side and rock face on the otherside and ate some chocolate to try boosting morale. Then, because that was so nice, a little later, in a very similar sort of layby, I had another bit. About 8 or 9 pm I admit to a touch of detached anxiety re survival chances – for there's nothing like motion when it comes to allaying fear, but the increasing cold, and queasy feeling from the chocolate on an empty stomach, was giving serious concern.

But then there came a tunnel, a hole in the mountain that lorries go through, and that's enough to make you wish you were still out in the rain, but this one had a road beside it, the old road, half buried, half overgrown – now a cycle track. It went round the mountain instead of through it. Then I was looking. Any place would do. A girl on a mountain bike came hurtling towards me and we missed each other by millimetres. Getting a fire going was my top priority. Before long I saw a pile of logs where a tree had fallen across and been cleared, near that there was a stream coming off the mountain; fresh clean water, seasoned logs and a thin strip of dirt to put the tent on at the head of an estuary. I quickly got a big fire burning, stripped off and got all my clothes, sleeping bag, everything hung out over a makeshift drying rack, made tea, ate a big meal. The sky cleared, the wind eased, the view was stunning . It was a good end to a bad day.

Tue 2 august

Everything was going fine, it was a clear day and for
a brief spell I had the wind behind me as I went
around the estuary below Olderdalen. Then battled
on up to Sorkjosen and on through Storslett. Quite
big towns with lots of supermarkets and people
hurrying around on bikes. Just as I was coming out of
Storslett I had my second puncture, the first of four
for the rest of the day. In truth the tyre had worn so
thin it was easy for anything to get through it. The
offending thorn had hidden itself obliquely in the

tyre and only showed when the tyre was pulled or pushed in the right way. The tyre was in a very bad state by the time i'd had it off several times. It had stretched a lot and the tube was poking through the side of the tyre wall. The only water available was a stagnant brook, I didn't use that. A nice German couple stopped and asked if I needed help. I politely declined. Eventually I swapped the front tyre with the back tyre to put less weight on the bad tyre. Because of all that I didn't get much further, but found a nice spot to camp and sort things out.

Wed 3 august

no punctures. Swapping the tyres and keeping the
pressure low seems to have cracked it. I met the
German couple again – late middle aged and going
quite slow. They were polite and friendly, but we
quickly ran out of conversation and they had to get
going again because it was too cold to hang around.
I saw them again at Bjurford because I stopped there
for lunch; he was carrying 40kg of gear ontop of the
bike. No wonder they're going so slowly I thought.
Bjurford looked good for fishing but it was too cold. I
went on to Langfjorden and camped there –
beautiful. Grass and then a stony beach with the
road behind some trees.

Thurs 4th

fish are jumping and gulls are going crazy in the
estuary when I get up so I take my telescopic rod
down through the weed covered boulders. It breaks
on the first cast. Two seals break through the
surface and gobble everything up till all goes quiet. I
go and make some tea and pack up the tent. Three
reindeer amble onto the beach as I sit with my tea,
one is albino. As I leave I see the Germans go past

and watch them grinding along on the flat. I watch them trail away out of sight then go brush my teeth at the stream that runs down to the beach. When I catch them up they're having one of their 2km breather breaks. 'Hello.' I call out to them. 'Caught you trying to sneak past while I was still asleep!' Silence. Then she said: 'No.' Muddling on from that was awkward, but they'd seen reindeer aswell and were enjoying the scenery so we parted amicably and I rode on determined to get well ahead of them this time. Infact, I reached Alta by early afternoon and went straight into the first supermarket I found, bought the usual things, bread, milk, rice, sausages, chocolate, liquorice.

I called in at the airport on the way north out of town to see if I could get a ticket. It was all quiet in there except the one fat bloke, unusual because you don't normally see fat people in Norway, infact he looked English, sitting there in his chair behind a desk. 'You must book online,' he said, 'it is 300 to 500 krona more if you buy here.' I wasn't sure if that was helpful or not. It felt like he was being helpful, but then he never left his chair.

Fri 5th

hanging around in Alta and bloody freezing. Tried two fishing spots with my repaired rod. Nothing. Very disappointing. The library was warm and friendly, I spent ages on the computer and printed out my tickets, but I couldn't spend 5 days there. So I went and bought a new tyre for £30. couldn't believe how cheap it was. How could a loaf of bread cost £4 and a tyre 30? the tyre was made in China.

Happy to be back on the road again in good weather I cycled about 10km out of Alta and found a nice little headland to camp with views back towards Alta and north to mountains. Past all the riff raff camped near the road outside of town. The tide's right out at midnight when I go to bed, and up sloshing around the rocks below the tent at five in the morning.

Sat 6th

not long now. Have I got time to go back up and see Porsangerfjorden north of Lakselv?

Will it be the same again? I'm asking myself but know i'm not going to bother. The weather's inclement at best. It's unlikely I'll see it in an orange glow like before. Probably it'll be freezing and grey. And I'm tired, all I want to do is some gentle cycling and fishing in a secluded area. Mull over the trip before the onslaught of travel again.

I turn left at Leibotn and head along the 883 to Storekorsnes. It's off the Norrkapp trail and just what I was after. A magnificent long descent to the coast again, with all the scenery under broken clouds. I catch some small pollock off the harbour wall, enough for a meal. Meet a nice old local guy at a cemetery who wants to talk but can't speak English. Poignant and human. Then I head back to a little spot by a river I'd seen earlier on, to camp and cook the fish.

Sun 7th

still here. Nice enough spot, lovely little stream that runs down off the mountain under the road and across the beach. It's a quiet road – a car goes by about every hour. I've washed my clothes and dried them all. Which has taken quite some time as it's cloudy and still; am sheltered here from the north wind which cuts across the edge of the beach at low tide. I've glued my shoes together, eaten bread and chorizo. Am beginning to think I should have bought new shoes. Anyway that's about it for today, gonna stay here walk along the beach, keep the fire going and listen to the waves ploshing against the shingle.

In the dream I had this morning, which is fading fast, I saw Antony, Jules, Richard and John, but I new other friends were there. We were waiting outside a church, about to go in for a service. I'd say a pretty unusual sort of service because great beds were being wheeled in instead of pews. Ever heard of going to church and lying in a bed? We were outside, about to go in and Antony said: 'I think I'll have another couple of these.' And he gets out a little packet of tiny cylindrical pills, dabs three of them one after the other onto his tongue with a cotton bud cigarette shaped thing. Then he did that disarming smile which starts with a little curl of the lip and broadens out into a massive grin. I said, 'Is that speed Antony?' 'Yes,' he replied, as amused by my bewilderment as I was shocked by his carte blanche style. Jules looked concerned as well, but said nothing. I think all the people around chatting and all the beds arriving were distracting him. But then his concerned look transmuted into the look of comradely responsibility; Antony's taking drugs so maybe I ought to as well, that way he won't be alone in there. The arriving congregation accepted the presence of the beds without evident surprise. And Richard went in to be helpful – rolling the beds in through the great doors, holding the doors open, chattering with all the colourful people, about this and that, how many wives or children they had, how many grandchildren. I went in and found him crouched down behind a headboard tightening up bolts. 'What's going on Rich? I mean, this is a bit weird isn't it?' And I was thinking about that stone circle mumming or speaking in tongues type of thing we stumbled upon at an ancient stone circle, how we couldn't stop ourselves laughing, how this might not be quite so accepting a congregation. I was crouched down next to him whispering, trying to get some sense out of him, he'd been mixing with these people, he should know something. 'What is it with all these beds Rich?' But he just calmly said that we had to help them bolt all the beds together so they didn't move during the service. Like everything was self evident. Richard is one of the most logical people I know so when he said that I felt even more worried especially considering Antony and Jules were now very likely to become unpredictable. And

I'm sorry but that's all there is. I'd have liked to have found out what happened as well. It was my dream after all.

Still sun 7th

now it's early evening , raining, nothing to do but lie in this tiny tent and write stuff, and maybe it's boring but that's tuff. What i've noticed about waving is that some wave first and some wait to be waved at before waving and some don't even wave at all. When that happens I wonder, all over again, if I actually exist; thinking and feeling aren't enough proof, there can only be conviction. I have to remind myself that some did wave, infact many people waved before I did and I take that as evidence that they're not only making a reciprocative human contact but are tacitly in sympathy with the nature of the adventure that I have been undertaking. The waving, especially waving first, is, I feel, a life affirming action. Not existing along with thousands of others is a heartwarming feeling.

In their defence, some of the don't even do that's have grudgingly said hello in reply to a repeated louder hello to make sure they've heard. Or a vigorous wave to make sure they've seen. Now, don't misunderstand me, I believe everyone has a right to wave or not. No one should be forced to wave. We'd all be living in fear. But what I've noticed about Norway, is that there are more first wavers. I haven't experienced the honking that I experienced in 2008 but maybe in the far north of Norway there aren't so many honkers. Or maybe honkers have given way to wavers. And there are all sorts of wavers – eager ones, ironic ones, conspiratorial ones... but my fear is, I have a fear that they're all going to give way to the don't even do that's. Everyone to stop waving. The reason I think that's possible is proximity. The less people one sees the friendlier they are. Ireland is an exception. Everyone's friendly but nobody waves. It's very confusing. After a while you get tired of saying hello, or your arm hurts and the waves dwindle to nothing. A swift and subtle shift from lots to nothing. One also retreats into the position of reluctance to wave incase 'they' don't. It feels a bit silly waving on ones own. A bit like unreciprocating love, it's humiliating, not to have ones wave returned, makes one feel a fool, a mad waving fool. Maybe for many that's part of the irony of the big wave. Such a wave is already anticipating zero return. But the problem with that is the being drawn into wave psychosis. Better not to wave or to choose ones wave carefully. You can usually tell who's going to wave and who isn't. The don't even do that's have got it written all over them. It's hypocrisy to wave to them.

But I think it is fear that is universally holding us all back from waving at each other. And it's a shame. I blame technology, loss of respect for elders, loss of values and decline of the church. Just when i've decided to overcome this fear and break out of my egotistical bubble somebody blanks me. Typical. Fills me with rage. How dare you blank me you arrogant, fashion conformist, clique mentality, sweaty handed swine. And that rage consumes me for at least 30 minutes, cycling along hurling a tirade against the landscape. So it's the rage that I find is most interesting. You've got to say that in a sort of pastors voice. Imagine you're an up and coming guru trying to make your way. Practice: how would you say – 'It is this rage that I find most interesting'?

Because it is just rage. That's all it is. Simple isn't it?
But this rage is, I think, becoming more common.
We are living in a time of epidemic rage. It's
connected with the waving, it's about rights, or lack
of rights, or it's sexual frustration – all the rich
bastards are getting it – but most of all it's a rage
against humanity for allowing people, children, to
starve, suffer, die while others live like kings. While
others justify themselves; hypocrite lecturers, smug
charity managers, doctors on huge salaries. And all
the others who think they deserve. It's a rage against
the self, against god for making the self. I think that's
why Steinbeck chose the grapes of wrath as a title,
for a cut throat era of winners and losers in a
heartless battle for market share; everyone tills their
own soil and makes their own destiny you say?
You're right. I was getting carried away there with
rhetoric. I don't believe in equality any more than
you do. I don't want foreign seeds in my carefully
tilled soil. At least i'd rather support a good looking
white kid than the brown progeny of those foul
Bulgarian beggars. After all, what value will it have
been taught? How to steal? Isn't it already on the
road to crime and destruction? But then we're in an

age of destruction, i'm told they are the agents, it's inevitable as the dark side of the moon or the collapse of socialism.

And it's a rage against that deep rooted feeling. It's a tribal rage against a cosmopolitan world. Be honest – underneath all the goody goody lefty stuff don't you feel this too?

Mon 8th

another wet day in the arctic circle. Visibility poor.
Using my waterproof to substantiate the tent where
there's a leak. Ate my last pack of Marie Kek biscuits
while waiting for the rain to stop. Left about 10
heading back towards E6. A pair of golden eagles
flew over me as i went around a steep sided inlet.
That would have been an award winning photo.
More rain fell and didn't stop. But i didn't complain –
I'd seen a pair of golden eagles close up. Shoes were
coming apart, the gluing hadn't worked so i had to
tie them around under the sole with the laces. Oh
and the wind changed so it was still against me.
Theres a big lake at the junction with the E6. I was
thinking about camping there but i couldn't see
anywhere that wasn't either wet or very private
looking or inaccessible. Lorries were thundering past
and my wet feet drove me on steadily to the top of
the mountain that climbed up from the plain north
of Alta. A little way down the road there was a fast
narrow river about 100m from the road. A steep
track led down to it. Beside it there was small birch
and heather near an old concrete bridge. I put the
tent there and built another big fire for drying,

which was all steam and smoke to start with —
pluming up into the cloud. The rain turned to drizzle
and i sat in that cloud, by the fire in my new slippers
made from bits of sleeping mat.

Nice Little Tea Party by the Sea

Just her and me. Lovely. Just how we liked it, sitting
out on the verandah, the old cast iron table laid out
with full silver. A nice linen table cloth and those
quaint frilly napkins she so liked. Iced tea — it being
so warm — and a slice of almond cake. Oh and those
little biscuits she used to buy. I used to say to her:
'Margery, you know you're going to bankrupt me
with those biscuits.' They were ridiculously
expensive. 'Oh, Henry you're such a cad,' she'd reply.

It was a balmy afternoon and we were sitting there
looking out over the bay, blissfully content as
always. We never had a crossed word. Margery and
I. infact, we never tired of each other. We could talk
for England on almost any subject, or we could sit
together in perfect silence, occasionally turning to
smile at each other. I had to admit, she always had
the best smile. Complete candour. That was what it
was. That was its winning charm. Mine wasn't so bad

either. Or so she told me. Ha, ha. 'Henry,' she'd say, 'you have a winning smile, you know that don't you?' I'd reply, 'I've no idea what you're talking about Margery.' And she'd laugh, that chirruppy, moneyed laugh.

But that afternoon turned out rather uncomfortably hot. Even so that the iced tea wasn't cooling it. And i was just about to say: 'Margery, i think we better go on inside, it's too hot out here,' when she leant forward, with the knife she used for cutting the almond cake, and stabbed me in the chest, right through my clean white shirt. When i looked down the shirt already had a big red blood stain on it and red spots were dripping onto the tablecloth. I was leaning forward, i said: 'Margery, you just stabbed me.' I was very shocked. I think she was as well because she looked quite alarmed. 'Henry, oh I'm so sorry, I really don't know how that happened..' Then i fell dead onto the table so i missed the rest of the sentence.

Now i know you're going to say: 'Thats ridiculous, you've lost all verisimiltude there, how can you possibly have died and still be telling the story?'

Well, I say: 'obviously it's all an elaborate fiction. Ha ha ha.'

tue 9th

only spaghetti left so i have that for breakfast. It's dry and cloudy. I cycle into Alta against a strong southerly wind. Straight into the big COOP for bread, milk, ham and prunes. Go into the airport to check that my printed ticket is valid. Outside the sun comes out and the mountains stand aglow in full splendour. I go to the Alta museum and rock carvings – ancient Sami pictures hewn into rocks near the sea. Worn faint but still visible. World heritage sight. Lots of french people taking photos. 6000 year old carvings of reindeer, fish, elk, canoes. Hard to see the stories in the pictures. But i like the language around them – gateway to another world, lower, middle, upper earth; Sami paradise, mother of creation, god of wind... The Sami gods seem more fickle than the one and only god, and that makes sense to me somehow. It connects with the thoughts i've been having about the wind being always against me. Call it egotistical but it feels like more than chance. Sometimes i can't help feeling, after having cycled in two directions against the wind, there's a hand sending me a message. I think of all sorts of possible messages which i won't bore you with and then cycle back into town, against the wind. It must be just chance. There are all the other people. The wind affects them too. And they're travelling in all different directions. Yes they are and some of them are the lucky ones, wind always behind them. There was a picture of one of those lucky ones in the museum. 50's, lent on the bonnet of his car. One of the Norwegian colonisers. A pretty girl on each side gazing adoringly at him, his hands rest lazily on them as he looks at the camera and smiles, a big smarmy smile of success. Now don't get me wrong – it doesn't trouble me, but as i looked at that picture i understood why the god of wind is against me: I'm a bad loser – i refuse to play.

Inland next to the Alta river, later on, i cook sausages and eat them with fresh bread, watch the salmon fishing boats motoring up and drifting back with the engine cut and fly lines glistening in the evening light.

Wed 10

still here cooking sausages over a little driftwood fire next to the river. Waiting here in my mocassins, i burnt one of the soles and was surprised how much black smoke it produced, feels good. Think i'll stay here. Apart from all the big general ideas, stocktaking that never happened because i was too tied up with the day to day beauty, decision making that never happened because i don't think it was necessary; apart from the conundrum of whether to uncamp from here and go into town to buy new shoes or live with these mocassins until i get to italy, the big question at the moment is what to do with the bike. There are some pine woods infront of the airport and it occurred to me i could hide it and cover it for a future trip. That way i could fly to Alta and start from there. But it would be rusty if it was still there. It didn't feel right. Or i could strip the bike of useful bits, e.g. Tyres, like i did with the last one. And then bin the rest. But i just like the idea of leaving the bike ready to ride. It feels inkeeping with the ethos of the trip. It makes sense. The bike was a gift and i'm leaving it as a gift. I don't think it needs a note.

Thurs 11

i wasn't going to write anymore as that seemed a
good place to end, but i don't know that this is over
until i tell you about how beautiful and how cold it
was when i packed up the dew wet tent at 1.30 and
set off into the orange glow of morning. Mountains
behind were dark shapes against the sky and the
mountains ahead across the fjord beyond the airport
were shining red. The roads were deserted. And the
wind was behind me. Way too early. Even going
slowly i arrived at 3 and the airport was all closed up
not a soul about. Into the woods to the tarp shelter
I'd found previously. Nobody around, too cold,
maybe they'd already gone south. I lit a small fire,
changed my socks and warmed my cold feet, first
one then the other, like that till 5. i left the bike
there with the repaired fishing rod still attached and
walked to the terminal. Goodbye Norway, not
forever i hope.

Bikes final resting place

Also by the Chris Deakins:

Poetry -

In a Parallel World, 2011, original plus

the angry woodcutter collection, 2014, Amazon.

'Well crafted...excellent poems.Highly
recommended.' The Supplement, Atlanta publishing.

Printed in Great Britain
by Amazon

56195553R00056